THE RAVENS OF FARNE

A Tale of Saint Cuthbert

by Donna Farley
illustrated by Heather Hayward

CONCILIAR PRESS
Ben Lomond, California

The Ravens of Farne: A Tale of Saint Cuthbert

Published by
  Conciliar Press
  (A division of Conciliar Media Ministries)
  P.O. Box 76
  Ben Lomond, California 95005

Printed in Hong Kong by Bookplus International Ltd

ISBN 978-0-9822770-5-8

12 11 10 09   4 3 2 1
1st edition, November 2009

Acknowledgements

Thanks to Bev Cooke, Linda Finlayson, and Katherine Hyde for their input on the manuscript;
to Heather Hayward and Carla Zell for fulfilling my vision of the Venerable Bede's story about Saint Cuthbert and the ravens;
and especially to Jane Meyer for her editorial enthusiasm and tireless work on this project.
Special thanks as well to Aidan Hart for his kind permission to reproduce the icon of Saint Cuthbert.

THIS BOOK IS FOR THEO
who like Saint Cuthbert loves all kinds of animals.

The man of God Cuthbert came to live
on the Island of Farne alone.
All alone with God
he meant to stay—
just Cuthbert, God,
and the birds of Farne.

Oh the birds that fed and nested on Farne!
   puffins and fulmars,
      terns and gulls,
   cormorants and eider ducks—

         linnets and pipits,
            warblers and sparrows
               . . . and a tribe of cheeky ravens.

The birds built nests
to hold their eggs,

and the monk built a place
to hold his prayers.

Across the deep water
sailed Cuthbert's friends,
   the monks of Lindisfarne,
to help him build his home.

From earth and stone they built his home:

a chapel to pray in by night and day;
a house where he could sleep and eat;
a garden patch, a freshwater well
. . . and around it all, a tall, tall wall.

Back sailed the monks to Lindisfarne.

Safe from the wind, inside the wall,
he planted his grain,
   drank from his well,
   and slept and ate and prayed.

Inside the wall, heaven was all
the man of God could see—
stars at night and sun by day . . .

. . . and the birds that flew overhead.

But then one day, oh what a surprise!
As Cuthbert picked his grain,
   down flew a flock of
      linnets and pipits,
         warblers and sparrows
           —and the bold
           and greedy ravens!

The man of God
     cried out to them, "Ho!
How dare you eat grain
     you did not grow?

"If God Himself has said you may,
I will give you leave to eat.
                But if not—

—if not, stop taking what is not yours
                and be off!"

                        And away they all flew—
                                linnets and pipits
                                        warblers and sparrows

                        —and last of all, the ravens!

One day in winter, Cuthbert's friends
came to visit Farne again.
When they towed their boats ashore,
their feet were chilled by the freezing waves.

Crowded into Cuthbert's hut,
the monks took off their soggy shoes,
crusted with salt from the sea.

With warm water the man of God
thawed their tingling toes.

"What we need," Cuthbert said,
"is a bigger house for guests!"

The monks of Lindisfarne agreed
and planned to help him build.

When next they came, they brought their tools
and timbers and roofing straw.

Soon they had built a house near the shore,
outside Cuthbert's wall.

But as the monks admired their work,
    down came the ravens cawing and crowing
        to raid the roof and snatch off the straw!

"Let that alone!" the man of God said.
But the ravens only mocked him!

So Cuthbert shouted, "Away with you, now—
In the name of Jesus Christ!"

Then bowing their heads in guilt and shame,
the ravens took to flight.

Three days later, while the man of God
weeded his garden rows,
one of the ravens returned.

Beak in the dust, he bowed down low,
with feathers all outspread.

"Well," said Cuthbert, "are you sorry, then?
If it is true, then you and your friends
have leave to come back again."

So the bird flew off.

Then back to Cuthbert's garden all the ravens flocked.
A gift they brought, a lump of lard, and set it at his feet.

Cuthbert cried, "How humble you are!
If only human folk would learn
to wash away their pride like this,
with prayers and tears and gifts!"

When next the monks were Cuthbert's guests,
he brought out the ravens' gift.

He helped them rub the lard on their shoes.
"Now this will keep the leather dry
whenever you launch your boats!"

For many years after, the ravens lived
on Cuthbert's island of Farne.

No longer stealing from him or his guests,
they made their nests
from island grass

and ate food they found for themselves. ◖

About Saint Cuthbert and the Farne Islands

Saint Cuthbert's Cross

Saint Cuthbert lived in the north of England in the seventh century A.D. He loved all of God's creatures. In the *Life of Saint Cuthbert*, Bede tells us the story of the ravens, as well as stories about the saint and other animals such as horses, eagles, and sea otters.

People in those days used to steal the fluffy down feathers from the nests of eider ducks. They made warm coverings for rich people, but the eider ducklings froze to death. When he became bishop, Saint Cuthbert made a law that no one must steal from the nests of these birds any more or harm them in any way.

Today it is also the law that people may not harm birds on the Farne Islands, where Saint Cuthbert used to live with the birds and pray in his little church.

Icon of Saint Cuthbert by the hand of Aidan Hart.

About the Author and Illustrator

DONNA FARLEY is a Word Guild Award winner for Canadian Christian Fiction. Her short stories have appeared in numerous anthologies and magazines in the US and Canada, including *Cicada* magazine for young adults. She has also published poetry and nonfiction, including the Conciliar Press book *Seasons of Grace: Reflections on the Orthodox Church Year*. Her next project from Conciliar Press, *Bearing the Saint*, is a young adult adventure novel set in the time of the Viking invasions, and will appear in 2010.

HEATHER HAYWARD would rather draw than do just about anything else. She produces artwork and illustrations for clients when she isn't busy doing illustrations for books. She has an Art degree from Western Washington University and a Graphic Design degree from Whatcom College. She resides in beautiful Lynden, Washington.